PIGGLES' GUIDE TO...

AIRSHIPS

BY KIRSTY HOLMES

©2019
The Secret Book
Company
King's Lynn
Norfolk PE30 4LS

ISBN: 978-1-912502-48-6

Written by:
Kirsty Holmes
Edited by:
John Wood
Designed by:
Danielle Rippengill

A catalogue record for this book
is available from the British Library.

All facts, statistics, web addresses and URLs in this book were verified as valid and accurate at time of writing.
No responsibility for any changes to external websites or references can be accepted by either the author or publisher.

Original idea by Harrison Holmes.

IMAGE CREDITS

CONTENTS

PAGE 4   Welcome to Flight School!

PAGE 6   Lesson 1: What Is an Airship?

PAGE 8   Lesson 2: Parts of an Airship

PAGE 10   Lesson 3: Inside an Airship

PAGE 12   Lesson 4: Lift!

PAGE 14   Lesson 5: Control!

PAGE 16   Lesson 6: Trip on an Airship

PAGE 18   Lesson 7: Famous Airships

PAGE 20   Flight Check

PAGE 22   Bonus Lesson: Skydive!

PAGE 24   Glossary and Index

WORDS THAT LOOK LIKE <u>this</u> CAN BE FOUND IN THE GLOSSARY ON PAGE 24.

WELCOME TO FLIGHT SCHOOL!

If you like balloons, but just wish they had a bit more power, then you've come to the right place! The Sty in the Sky Flight School!

STY IN THE SKY
ACADEMY
EARN YOUR WINGS

Here, you will learn all you need to know about some amazing flying machines, and join the **elite** flying force known as the Pink Wings! So pay attention: it's time to FLY!

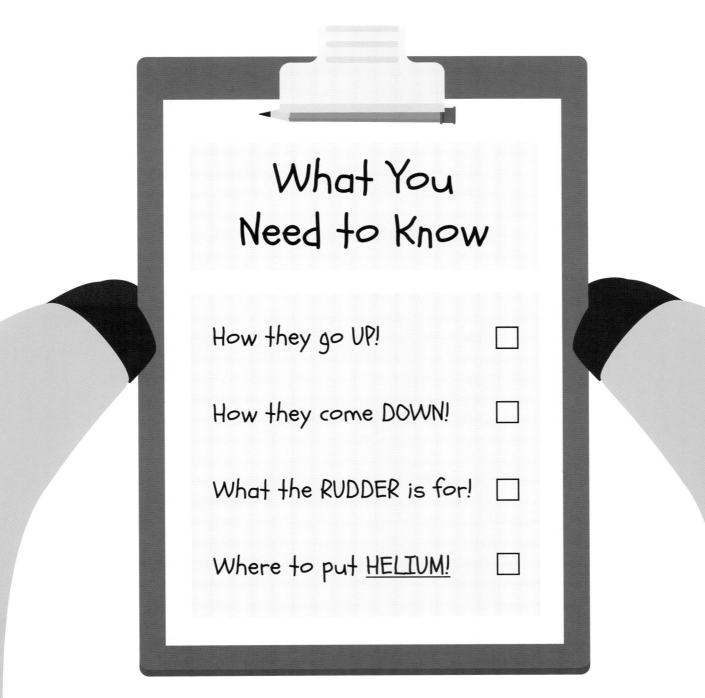

What You Need to Know

How they go UP! ☐

How they come DOWN! ☐

What the RUDDER is for! ☐

Where to put <u>HELIUM!</u> ☐

Lesson 1: WHAT IS AN AIRSHIP?

Airships are a type of lighter-than-air (LTA) aircraft. They weigh less than the air around them, so they float – just like a balloon!

Airships, or blimps, are different to balloons because they can be controlled and steered, using engines and propellers.

LESSON 2:
PARTS OF AN AIRSHIP

MOST AIRSHIPS LOOK LIKE THIS, AND THEY ALL HAVE THE SAME BASIC PARTS.

Let's look at the parts of an airship.

PIGGLES

RUDDER
This steers the airship.

ENVELOPE

This is a large bag filled with helium.

BALLONETS

Large bags inside the envelope are filled with 'heavy' air.

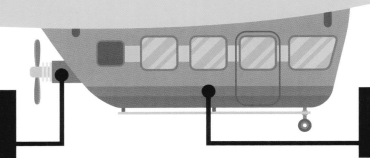

ENGINE

This provides power and control.

GONDOLA

This carries the crew and passengers.

LESSON 3:
INSIDE AN AIRSHIP

COMPASS
Shows Direction

MAP
Shows Location

ALTIMETER
Shows Height

MONITOR
Shows Helium Levels

The cockpit is at the front of the gondola. The pilot sits here and uses **instruments** and controls to fly the airship. They tell the pilot about height, direction, weather and wind speeds.

The passengers travel in the **rear** of the gondola. Cabin crew look after the passengers during the flight. Often, there is just one cabin crew member and they sit in the cockpit with the pilot.

LESSON 4:
LIFT!

Lift is a **force** that pushes things upwards. Airships use lighter-than-air helium gas to create lift. The helium makes the envelope, and the airship, float.

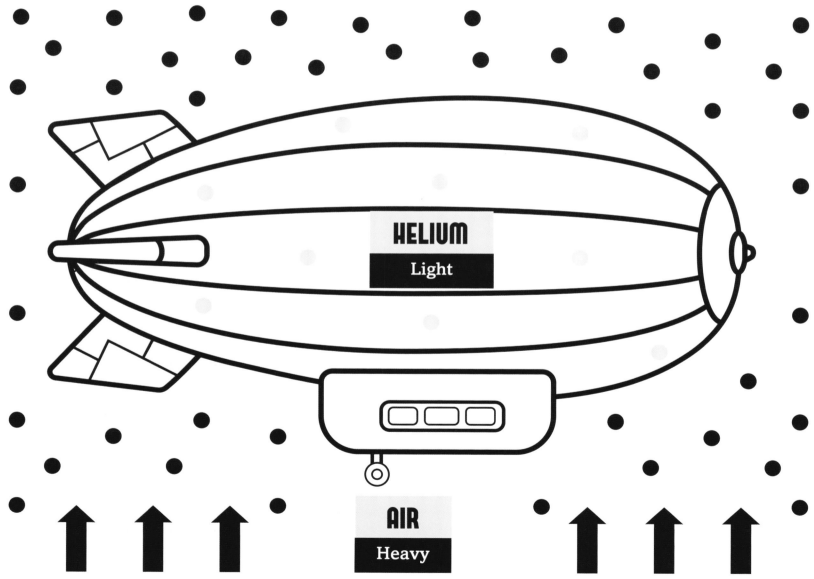

HELIUM
Light

AIR
Heavy

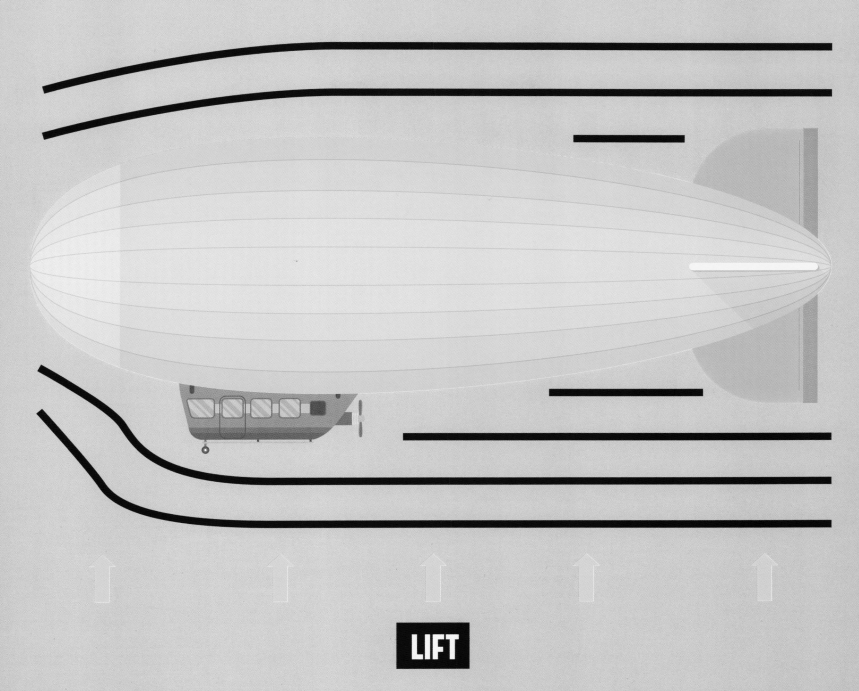

LIFT

The oval shape means air can pass easily over it, making it easier to **manoeuvre** (say: man-oo-ver). Some airships are soft, and use the gas to keep their shape, while others have **rigid** frames.

LESSON 5:
CONTROL!

L

Propellers are like huge fans.

RIGHT! RIGHT!

Airships can move forwards, left and right. Propellers on the sides push the airship forwards using a force called thrust. The rudder at the back controls the air flow, steering the ship.

14

Airships can also move up and down. The helium lifts the airship up; but how do they move down?

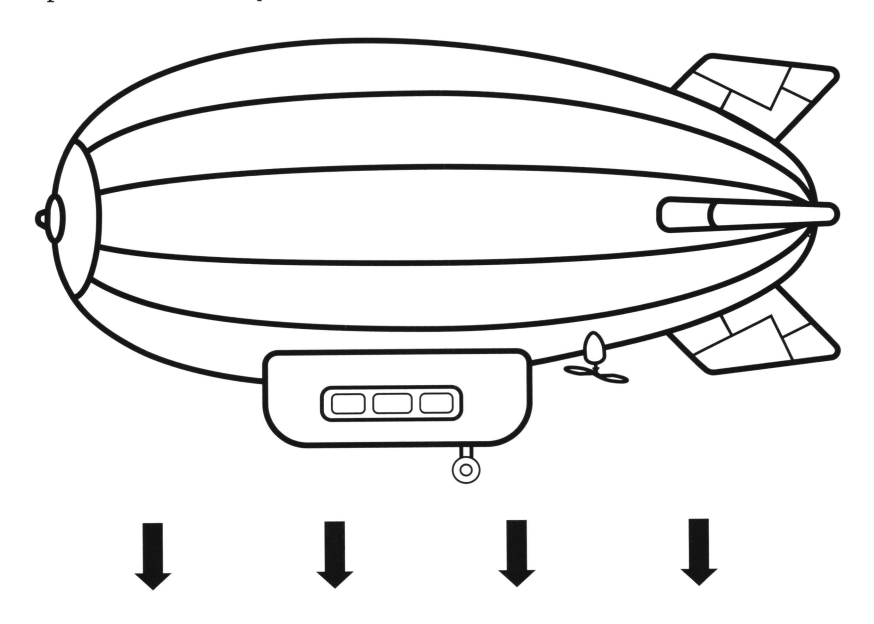

The pilot fills the ballonets with air, which is heavier than the helium. The propellers turn to point down, creating downwards thrust.

LESSON 6:
TRIP ON AN AIRSHIP

To let passengers on and off, the pilot carefully balances the airship close to the ground. The ground crew put a ladder to the door and passengers 'swap' one at a time – one on, one off.

Airship flights are amazing. Every seat is near the window, and most airships only fly at around 50 kilometres per hour (kph), so there is plenty of time to enjoy the view!

LESSON 7:
FAMOUS AIRSHIPS

THE HINDENBERG

German airship, the Hindenberg, was one of the largest airships ever flown. It flew passengers across the Atlantic Ocean and was destroyed in a famous fire.

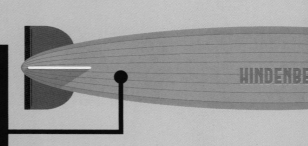

HINDENBERG

THE 'FLYING BUM'

The Airlander 10 is the largest airship in the world. It is 92 metres (m) long, 43.5 m wide and can travel at 148 kph. Its curvy shape earned it the nickname 'the Flying Bum' or the 'Butt Blimp'.

AIRLANDER

THE GOODYEAR BLIMP

The Goodyear Company in the USA has been using blimps in their advertising since 1925. This famous blimp is often seen at sporting events.

GOOD YEAR

NEW MAP CREATED FOR THE ARCTIC

LZ-127

GRAF ZEPPELIN

ARCTIC ZEPPELIN

A Graf Zeppelin flew a team of scientists to the North Pole in 1931, taking photos and creating a new map of the Arctic.

FLIGHT CHECK

OK, students. Let's test your knowledge about airships and see if you've been paying attention! Get them all right, and you earn your Pink Wings!

Questions

1. Which is heavier – helium or air?

2. What does the rudder do?

3. Which instrument shows the airship's direction?

4. Which force pushes the airship up?

5. What is the nickname of the Airlander 10?

Did you get all the answers right? You did? Well done!

This means you are now an expert **aviator** and you have become a member of the world's most elite flying force: The Pink Wings!

SKYDIVE!

It takes a lot of training to fly an airship; there are fewer airship pilots in the world than astronauts! Pilots have to know how to launch and land safely, and what to do in an emergency...

STEP ONE
Identify Emergency

"WHAT'S THAT SMELL?"

STEP TWO
Don't Panic

STEP THREE
Grab Parachute

STEP FOUR

Evacuate!

...and always know where the emergency exit is!

GLOSSARY

AVIATOR   someone who flies an aircraft

ELITE   someone or something which is the best of a group

FORCE   a power or energy

HELIUM   a gas which is lighter than air

INSTRUMENTS tools or devices for doing a job

MANOEUVRE   steer and control a vehicle

REAR   the back end of something

RIGID   hard and not flexible

INDEX

BALLOONS 4, 6–7

ENVELOPE 9, 12

GONDOLAS 9–11

HELIUM 5, 9–10, 12, 15

HINDENBERG 18

LIFT 12–13, 15–16

PILOT 10–11, 15–16. 22

PROPELLERS 7, 14–15

STEERING 7–8, 14